STACK

stack

James Davies

CARCANET

First published in Great Britain in 2017
by CARCANET PRESS Ltd
Alliance House, 30 Cross Street
Manchester M2 7AQ

A CIP catalogue record for this book is
available from the British Library.

ISBN 9781784104863.

Book design: Luke Allan.
Printed and bound in England by SRP Ltd.

The publisher acknowledges financial
assistance from Arts Council England.

Supported using public funding by
ARTS COUNCIL
ENGLAND

stack

First published in Great Britain in 2013
by CARCANET PRESS Ltd
Alliance House, 30 Cross Street
Manchester M2 7AQ

A CIP catalogue record for this book is
available from the British Library

ISBN 978 1 847771 016

Book design: Tony Ward
Printed and bound in England by SRP Ltd

The publisher acknowledges financial
assistance from Arts Council England

rocks[1]

walked into a bar

didn't a roof

i was holding a bit

i had a broken bit of skirting

stair-rod too

a loud bang

a red big bus

morning following early

———————————————

rocks[1]

on a rock

a hedgehog

leaves

comes

sellotape

a huge thing

i like to walk in a field

the skys

lime

8

o'clock

leaning next to a grapefruit

bought an electrical item with the wrong lead

crushed a snail

talking to a brick

thinking about a shed

some times a month

bird||||||||||||||||||||||||||||||||||||||||||||||||||||no bird

three | square | alarm | clocks

white green blue

white | green | blue

green white blue

rocks[1]

piglet jumping

glass twix

9 petals

turned the sound down on a video, minimised the tab and left it running

9 hours and then started another one

_____

1 rocks

shouldn't i be outside watching a snail

what have you got there for lunch

to use paint but not make paintings

jug[1]

2 buddhas make same soup

one makes it differently

the sea is blue

white green blue

the sea is blue

_____

1

green white blue

my hat is yellow

little birds can be brown

that little blue bird is brown

that little bird *is* brown

i moved a seat

no fox[1]

i sat in the wind on a 10-ft rock and dropped a big blue ball

she danced on a box named d4

ambivalent sensations with a tiny orange cube

with electric fans behind her hair

a theatre of orange plastic biscuit-tin lids

a room of oracles

no fox[1]

charlotte re-finished the sculpture

aerial view of meteor crater, arizona

intergrown pyrite cubes

secret square with 1 line drawn

what is more than 'i had painted a twig'

it's the caravans i like in the picture

a pot near the top

sideways on to a lid

a photo of you eating lunch

a picture of me saying all the tobacco's run out

a pebble and a red moon

a man holding an electrical box

looked at a dustbin

a patch on a tile to the right

a girl standing next to a yellow stripe

charlotte re-finished the sculpture

a paintbrush by the shore to represent a painting of a paintbrush
by the shore

through a flap into a silver room

hovering oblongs

those two are the most important bollards to me

a lemon painted yellow

walked the beach alone saw a courgette[1]

---

goes out for hotdogs

at a total mountain and two boxes

low   /   orbs   /   birds   /   threads

a pile for lemon and lime skins

a woman just walked past carrying a bag

a pile of lemon and lime skins

the photo of it is in a box in the attic

and i got up

predictably we are sitting by a box

16

so i got up

wrote about a small pigeon

after drinks

ice

tess or like tess

a witness to a lemon on a slag heap

hit leg on that ledge

after lunch

ice

tess or called tess

something like a curtain

at a whereabouts

i have painted some string as close as possible to a cucumber

she smiled

at a packet of beef

went near a bench

saw a bicycle

in a shop

a man did not trip up in front of me

i have been in a room again

lifting a lid

i knew a patch

wanted to put a leaf in a box

when you stand on this square you become immortal

a sponge tubbed

enough beak for you to notice it as beak

a decision in four cushions

framed by a gap

hidden by three string bits

i tried to put a lid on a cup but i missed

a lot

then two squares coloured in

four tiles

3 donkeys 1 elephant

1000 goats

walked around with bells

walked around without a blue pen

important yellow patch under total glass floor for adoration game

tummy flat legs up and crossed hands and elbows propping up head

left 1 felt-tip in the pot

1 felt-tip in the post

left 1 pot in the felt-tip pen pot

a felt-tip sealed in an envelope with a postage stamp unsent

4 places

4 pink caps

4 more places

4 pink caps again

4 pink caps again

4 more places again

i thought it might be a good idea to do a drawing of some blue tac

the roof of a shed

rocks[1]

in the top room it is a pleasure

learned about a dog wastebin

1

should i had a nectarine before i go to bed

listened to a buttercup

attached 2 stickers

2 dots

9 lines

computer stuff in a computer bag

day-old lime cake was a story about a cracked CD case

a fondle in the replenishment area

hotel room when climbing over a fence

heather-fall

that is to say i could see crystals in a weather-beaten box

used a felt-tip pen

compare 'where'm i gonna put this half pack of batteries' with 'where did i put that half pack of batteries'

a reaction to a pink line

the same eucalyptus

a feeling towards plastic

meditation on sulphur, calcite and stibnite

went humbly by a leaf

by the cold of the moon

a pile of grass sticking out

i carry this secret to the grave

impossible exercise with ball

the drawing shows an amount of people by a bag of apples

didn't do what was possible with some bark

i saw her pencil on a tile

i saw her eat a lime

behind a wall

with a t-shirt

frontways to a beach

i have been in a car in the snow

a conversation whilst throwing sellotape

come round this bin

déjà vu on a bit of plastic

looked at a dustbin

singled out a box

is a rusty pan filled with what looks to be petrol

was a deep orange canvas called yum

pigtails and mushrooms

on a bicycle bridge 4:20 was light blue to very light blue

walked up a mountain

on and on

a repeat of that walk under the pergola

a photograph of your expression as you exit the store

one and one

i'm at home wearing new trousers and making intuitive drawings oh such a lovely   roof

3 oblique forms (february)

1 and 2

what is box

what is more i had painted a twig

what is that water jug for

2 and 1

mountains   at last

she caught me off-guard with a pair of beige trousers

already no more still here

the scent of a crab inside a rum and coffee

'the scent of a crab inside a rum and coffee' is simply another way
of saying that a bald tyre is a rectangular blue polyfoam

like the way i was outside mike's autos

turkeyfatsnow

something found behind a stack of palettes

come round this side of the bin

something i found behind a stack of palettes

a coaster may seem outdated but what if it had a nice picture on it

8 plastic cubes marginally misaligned

a bulb of pears

when towel bulb damp

an infinite amount of things in a finite system

a blink of gloam polished to a cigarette

i met him the following week

with a damp towel

9 am distant train

12 am moonlight

30

3 am outside here

7 pm shrine

5 am sunrise / sparrow beats

singing by a lid

by an until

look at that shed

next to a lid

red aurora

a translucent bee

a bridge

a pack of embassy no. 1s

of a curve (*that it is warm*)

in the dream the chair had been moved

a bit[1]

this bit is a called a carpet

a bit[1]

a blue glass ball

study of blockie

lime off cairn

this time the moon

a little bit

butterflies

blue poison dart frogs

in the morning both sing

a picture of the hut

6 irregular forms

mostly a box

conversation with magic square sequence

white marble form frosted with brick

at a slope down to a bit

varnished butternut squash

2 electric boxes

three toothbrushes sinking in a can of day-glo orange paint

hut in the woods

hats on a barge

white   .   green   .   blue footpath   .

light   lights

tiger

4 chairs

a wall   an orange

i cleaned a bowl

a retrieved object (an oblong)

i move towards the stapler and look at·it

concentration on a his and hers mug

i saw her again

being intimate with a brick

4 huge colourful planks

plinth

beside me

a set of small beads

cups

pink cat on black

openwindowbrickslampshade

red shiny skip

i like the look of those old boxes

i saw a man with a bag of bread

second movement round an imaginary miniature lemon

sitting

i noticed her about that lid

moving

1

sun   :   hazelnut

moon   .   raving

moon   .   still

a simple set of poles in polystyrene

yet another little wooden bridge with neon blue

in some woods

red with lamp post

a pot off the top

sometimes i have beach

teaspoons

come round this other side of the bin

20 differently coloured blocks in 20 identical pots

singled out a bench

what is meant by painting a brick

bird to consume

taking something out of something too quickly

painting   a teabag

we all had a good look at the orange table

we all had a good laugh at the orange table

this is a hatch in one of your old buildings

where stones are set amongst thousands of other stones

act 1: marcel duchamp   act 2: carl andre

mountains are high

rivers are wet

had a couple of beers

a continuity from blocks

VHS and technology boxes haphazardly

VHS and technology in a stack

how do you choose a brick

or whether a curtain

an object a day how much

room with a packet

room with a electric fire

room with a block

some tuna on the floor

looked at a tub

blue sun on yellow sky

returning to the bucket i noticed a leaf

greener damper summer

tables

some noodles with a bit of tuna in it and a bit of fluff

one left in a ten pack

that star is called something different

by a pack of ham

a white round room with red, yellow and blue curtains

when you stand on this square you become a bird

tuna in a dustpan

a hairdressers that is shut

a family chicken bucket which is served

a glass hi-fi cabinet door that won't quite shut with a tab

a computer monitor on a landing

a bit of plastic near a pigshed

drawing a circle with a straight line

soundtrack for man handing rental keys back in

the phone directory was in the hallway

i'd like to do a drawing of you with some AA batteries next to you

space for a thumbnail drawing of a donkey

half blockie on the side of a ordinary path

in the gallery

blackbird

dabs

bicycle barrier

a place in a place to make it not that place

electronic bells over a rock

i enjoyed being round at your house

near not daylight

drew a glass of apple juice

secret gesture with an stick

someone gave me a slip marked 'five red apples'

i forced her to look at a three-pin plug

at a grass touching experience

block   .   pillar   .   slab   .   beam

the day we did that role-play about a clothes horse

45

standing next to a biscuit

4 journeys round a box

was a girl crouching down looking at something in the grass

a bit

coffee throw

i drew a line at a beaches

representation of a project involving red yellow green and blue
canisters

it is possible to throw some grass up in the air

i stood next to him a bit

at a swimming pool

i liked that bit of plastic

more mountains

colour successions like red–yellow–blue

some doors piled up

i stood by some 1-foot wooden blocks

moved my hand slightly

not in a box

by a tub

secret code for kerb slabs

in a sports hall there is a bit of fluff

nudged a chair leg

hid a stone on top of another stone

moved a piece of tissue next to a column a bit

wittered to a hedge

she shocked me by a shed

that plank is a bit rough

17, 16, 15 (sunk), 14

cups

put myself in position of i was wearing a bright red baseball cap
cycling by a bright yellow field

experiment with doorstopper

5 clear acrylic cubes on paving slab

left the potato masher out in the garden overnight

posed as a girl selling strawberries at market

electronic puffs falter earliest to a part beach

red red blue

invention of blue metal bar

a mime about tilting a pack of compost slightly

stage curtain with a pushing motion

no block red shining

a boulder can show you another boulder then it's gone

files called 12 and 14 ways of not looking at a tub

around a piece of brown wool

yellow patch on total blue

rubber protective wire casing sample on display board

party with a log

i saw a girl wearing a scarf in the bank

a drape is an association

a field is near a public telephone box

adjustment of quantity of water in bucket (for *bucket composition 2*)

i watched

a party without a log

on a beach

with a formation

sunset in this place is even stronger

a sink bracket but only a bit

arrangement of cuboid acrylic rods orange orange orange blue

orange orange orange orange blue

2-cm chimpanzee model on 3-ft plinth

fluorescent brick in blacked-out room

design for 2 ashtrays

at a graduate or corporate fair

i went over to the garage for some snacks

a yellow scrap may be of importance

she gave me a towel to use in the bathroom

i saw one of those bins they attach to a lamp post

seafrontstarfruit

curtain

partly using a sink bracket

a system of black dice-sized cubes between different things

iron frame with orange tinted glass rectangular box 12x1x1

work in four parts   a brick   a path   a sky   a storm

clark coolidge is a found word from clark coolidge's 1967 collection
clark coolidge

wasn't a bucket by the shed

wasn't i with a bucket by some flytipped rug

the her wastebin

i saw a cracked CD case against a sunlounger

went left then forwards then right then forwards and so on
vanishing each time a sideways move occurred

sparrow   chrome pole things

lemon   yellow

behind the wall there is a box but you can't see it

three birds   a magpie   a pigeon   a seagull

snowflakes   i climbed to a vantage point

a piano only outsiding melancholy

8 balls

got to the same distance as him with a tub

the first 1000 google images of yellow paper cups 28/4/13

you're not allowed to go on that bandstand

a decision to remember all of them which way up

wood with a piece

big cabinet

string thing scudged with bollard

4 lights

red purse

with a packet of rice

a thing that goes back a bit

yellow partly

three birds   a magpie   a pigeon   a seagull

fold   up   chair

4 nights

stops[1]

almonds

2 green tabletops wrapped in cellophane

a room with only a bit of red

4 yellow rods

plastic structure with painted string and china piece

4 people in a line

2 women

orange glass lid for covering cheeses

_____

1 stops

glove compartment

mud on each part

it's a really exciting place with wooden things

table with no plum

out the back   /   in the snow   /   there is a guitar

a boat|||||||||||||||||||||||||||||||||||||||||||||||||||a boat

i bought a candle at the shop

2 clothes horses

a house

i met him with a carrier bag of leeks

red

twig and plastic exercise

a bit of plastic

almonds

cement   bags   left

orange pot

later then about

transparent orange, red and blue, all look right in any order how is a small plastic set against the landscape

i went for a walk on a tuesday

steam   .   .   .

a pie dish left out

a row of plug sockets bracketed against a white brick wall, 2 sockets
with plugs in (second and third in from the left)

a table which is almost unusable due to wetness

red shiny magic box

a sellotaped cube sequence

a bird in the tree a sun

how is this shell next to this other shell

a room with lots of flowers in it

a lot of rice

motorbike and man holding yellow patch next to it for photo

16 t-shirts

a box that opens up and contains a colour

a bit of rock

green china

a mat

sky

rocks[1]

yellow   black

put a wrapper on my bed for a second that i found inside

yellow   black

a shower fitting two-thirds up

17 years since

a string of rocks

there is a problem with an envelope

raininglight

a brick

i placed a spoon on top of another spoon and it fell off

i coloured in a whole sheet of standard white paper in blue using a blue crayon

darklight

i tried to focus on a thought of a carpet and it worked

in the chair

some blue tarpaulin covered a bit of grass

18 plastic boxes   variable sizes   with lids clipped shut filled halfway up with cotton wool on a 6-tiered shelving unit: metal x-bracket / plastic-coated hardboard, with wooden-look finish

4 white wooden spinning discs on a floor turning 4 glossy painted
bricks (blue red yellow green) back and forth 90°   it takes 2
seconds for the turn, at intervals of 2 minutes

i remember reading joe brainard during the week in the comfort of
my own home at a decent time of the day

went walking

behind a sofa

woods/woods

14 years since

i sat in a chair

i saw an organ when a beach

a room with a box in it

in a row 3 small metal balls a cube of wood a piece of plastic
shattered from a milk crate

i remember reading joe brainard during the weekend in the comfort
of my own home at a decent time of the day

a dog

3 taps

blue and red and, between, 2 other colours which could also be
blue and red

a train

examine the difference between a blue plastic put next to me and
placing myself next to a blue plastic

a disc the wrong way round

2 yorkshire terrier figurines

a video of a woman's walk from a piece of yellow plastic to a piece of orange plastic

light blue painting

big orange case which stores bright-orange disc which is missing

a rock

in the snow   /   out the back   /   there is a guitar

i painted a square red then blue then red again

it is impossible to have an artwork at an airport

5 red marbles one of which is unnecessary

47 pigeons

the first 1000 google images of big rocks

i went out

set up a stall for afternoon tea in my house with no one there, no drinks, no food, no tender, no chairs, no table, no music, no cake-stands

i looked for a section of the glass

great point in a swimming-pool place

a room with a clock and a sofa how would i approach it

a pot turned the wrong way up

take a look at these 3 oranges

i only came for a box

3 rocks that don't take up much space

on a table

deep white catering tray KB3

i decided to take another look at the orange couch

dropped my fork on the way to the curtains

hops around 30

synthesized piccolo to a window

no bucket amongst many buckets

piglet frolicking

rocks on a rug

inside a shed

faces

took a golf ball to work

lemon

8 years since

we did it by a mirror

the rectangular bits are gone

went to different places in the house for a break

2 trees

2 more lids

i arranged a box

a rock that goes on   a   bit

green china lamp base

we all had a good lift of the orange table

hole in skirting board for television wiring to pass through

2 rocks

walked past 34 stacked chairs and unstacked one of them

i put my hand up near a plastic box

we did it in the park

tripped over a brook

octagonal yellow ashtray

near a bush

15 years since

throughed

leaf sizing

tea | bags

there is no space round something on a wall

a tub the same size

43 accessories

grass near a late entrance

going upstairs i was puzzled

should i count each step a unit

rocks[1]

the snow fell in a place

i sat down in the grass

_____

[1] 1

restored an object

i lifted a box

fell asleep with a cube

fountain (a nice one)

i drew a fox in the same box as a duck

i can feel my arm

2 jugs

i saw a fountain on a beach

next to some stones

lots of beach

wood

a piece of metal

outside a bottle

rocks[1]

slipped walking up a ramp

a room with some flowers in it

i went into a room and had a look about a bit

two sticks represented a chinese gondola next to a mountain

1

drum machines apart

2 doorstoppers

1 rock on a rug

oblong a quarter and 3 quarters

lengthways

red patch against blue sky

a long room once

orange cloth slightly

i saw an organ with a bench

cup accident

a 1½-litre bottle of shampoo

pink

brick   /   paper   /   pen   /   amounts

a tree or thereabouts

2 windows

3 surfaces

a forest in the woods

i have opened this box for you

in a quarry

stopped

by a laptop

a lager can in half

shoddy but not in the mud

a re-enforced box

a set of tubs

a hut of sex

the same thing with the door

stood

on a step

a photograph of a tiger-striped bin

a photograph of a someone in a kitchen

stopping

jumping

in a field

put on an apron for the day

no one knows where the egg is hidden in the house or that it's in
the house or that it's hidden

the first 1000 google images of nice tubs

a pink line thickly

a rock

i put myself in front of a trowelhead

i went up to him and said 'butterfly'

rocks[1]

a butterfly

3 clear perspex cubes in their foam spaces

yellow and plank

balls

green green green

a sheet of glass with little wooden balls on top

out the back   /   there is a guitar   /   in the snow

i have only given you this red square from 4

a bicycle and bucket dismantled

a box for only 10 seconds

a visit to a shop selling plugs

i wrapped up some plastic for unwrapping later

i got a nice bird colouring-in and did it in brown

at first it was too hot then it was not

27th...

alex   drank   tea

heard the crickets

saw a swallow

lids everywhere

i did something on a desk

it felt clear it was not a tub

rocks[1]

goat and cricket

balls going round

2 blue rods against 2 blue logs

4 rocks in a kind of V

i asked a friend if i could push him for a plum

rocks 2:30

fence 3:31

ridge 3:43

1

2 plastic rods against 2 plastic logs

3 greens

5 grass away

absence of butter

round a corner

i danced with an apple

i walked over to his house to have a chat with him

we looked at a tree

touched a yellow mat on the floor

4 forks

1 knife

6 beers

no wine

i threw the last one away

a gilt framed photo of having an altercation with

a nice step half a mile away from a hardware store

a set of chairs but less

a part of that fence is 20 cm long

no lifting of the brush in the paint a buddha competition

i touched a bath

wet chickens

pens

a thing that appears which is never removed

rocks[1]   [1]rocks

2 green tubs

slide

i rolled a wooden cube on a rock

arriving there was only 1 box

brick for brick sculpture

1 rocks

man tripping as he lifts a yellow box

2 days with a piece of wood which has piece of wood written on it

an egg hidden swapped in an the eggbox

not enough glass on a fence 8 hours on

house north wales

we all had a good laugh with the orange table

25 red, 16 light green, 12 purple, 10 yellow, 8 dark green, 7 black, 8 brown, 9 blue, and 10 orange

3 minutes by some off-cut lino timed by a stopwatch

i asked a friend if i could push him for a plum

i defaulted on my arrangement and only used 3

an achievement in 4 stages

an arrangement outside on a table

by a crabshell

between 30 and 50 yellow lines

the ball stopped moving

i drew a picture of a red patch and filed it

i asked a friend if i could push him by a plum

i sat with him by a box

come and sit by this crate with me

as soon as i sat on the palette i smashed it up but then i saw a bus

red yellow green and blue follow in more or less that order

one of those long ones

one between 5 and 10

a lamp with stickers

i asked a friend if i could push her for a plum

lickingraining

3 kg

2 dogs

lime[1]   lemon[2]   pavement[3]

too many objects round a piece of plastic

there is a guitar   /   out the back   /   in the snow

table with 4 chairs

a box

_____

lime[1]   lemon[2]   pavement[3] halfway down

in about the middle

2 bricks gathered up and moved towards a table

i drew 1000 amazing images of teal

i went for a walk on tuesday

hid behind a thing

table exclusion

this plum starts here by this fir tree

stones

large jars

tab for glass cabinet coming off

a fantasy on a log

put a wrapper on my bed for a second that i found outside

what's inside that box

reconstruction of a plate

limping by a nut

that pole is by something else

i used a log with him

by those big white containers

buckets and chairs

4 forks 1 knife 6 beers no wine

i ate a grapefruit at a rock

red,yellow,green,blue,

i set up the piece of paper

i asked a friend if i could push him as a plum

broken and unbroken rocks

at marked lines there and there i consecrated a line

chairs

standing too close to a lift

i had someone hold an axe up for me, then place it on the mantelshelf

yellow or blue but never at the same time or in quick succession

i got a bit of glass caught in the sole of my foot

i took it out

a set of office blinds (orange)

a tub between

a screw top the side of

a shed

new hinge old bucket

i went towards a leaf

half in a yellow acrylic mesh lying sideways two-thirds down head out

establishment of stars

boys think about bark

wood with a stamp

i felt the underside of a slate whilst

a leaf to the door

i went in and out of the shop

i went to the record shop and then on to a friend's house

fiddled with my keys differently

3 cars

an extra lid

stairs

the mountain

says an expensive plate

a plum atop a lidded tub

i still used a drawer

and licked a shoehorn

and tubbed a lid

the radiator was detached

parallel to a diagonal benson of hedges

went to a different place with the same dustbin

event at a large memory foam pet bed leaflet

a box that couldn't be moved on the fourth occasion

8 x the white bird, 4 x the dark hill, 2 x the dark sea

only 2 stones on the table today

i had it near you

by a motel

i will do that gesture with you in 5 days' time

again

wooden bits a tub

i walked around a tree the wrong way

i searched around for my keys on the table

i had a thing

near a bit

for a minute and 3 seconds

then i went back into the room again

near a bit

a small foam falling a short distance

large white catering tray KB5

a mountain does not move

rope window

i did a space with a chair

with a bit of something

i didn't eat a biscuit by a window

with a beautiful clock

i bought a packet of cigarettes for her

white blue gold

a lid including a rotating office chair

we were about to walk down a ramp

bath

almonds

yellow

sofas

a polar bear, a lake, a mountain, the sun

the polar bear is looking at the sun

sun

suns

i pretended i was performing a play in a hut

stars[1]

a bit of rubber tubing

_____

with 29 other things

white white blue

a painting of 2 bricks from *equivalent viii*

what does that 'twisting' motion represent

i tried to walk towards a cheese sandwich

for 5 minutes

tubs used in different ways

over the edge of a glass covering

a bit to the left

i organised some people round to do a painting of a lawrence weiner statement

i organised some people round to do a painting of a mike nelson statement

brick throwing competition

on every staircase at some point

a bit of space to get through

into a house

2 images of blue

a yellow sponged

a new message coming through to a duck

i left a bit of my lunch

i asked a friend if i could push him with a plum

i've got a cauliflower here what should i do about that

walked through his zone of bin (the ashtray bit on top)

a box on top

a pot for what

a pot

3 windows

a painting

imagining a match

rock   and | rock

tea spoons a duck

fetching

a carpet

2 trolleys

somewhere in london

a great thing in half

a picture of an attendant telling someone to stand back a bit a shed roof

a pipe in fact

somewhere in london

white green blue

half a pencil

tights around the floor with a bit of music

sideways to a beach

a cup around the back

i think it's about time you got rid of that box

a page with cuckoo written down around 10 times

4 actors required

3 o'clock

no sea

only sea

i did a lead pencil drawing of white green and blue

ducks

green white blue

the sea

on the left

on the right

a machine round the back

a pool of water

worked out a plan by a duck

i drank a cherry coke by 2 bins 2 miles apart

2 on top of a lot

the fifth mushroom was hot

3 cherry cokes

took the lift

20.........30.........40.........50 cms away from a rock

toys got between a fence

i took a teaspoon to work

a tub full of plums

a sculpture

it's an otter

blew 3 things in a water-filled box

followed a drawing of a fox

followed a leaf by walking away from it

in a wood

water   .   a bird   .   a leaf   .   rocks[1]

a tub for a change

that towel isn't the right one

2 rocks on 1 rug

i couldn't sit on a ledge with him

near a chain

a decision to forget all of them which way up

_____

1

ACKNOWLEDGEMENTS

Some parts of *stack* appeared in *department*, *The Journal of Writing in Creative Practice*, and *Junction Box*. Other parts appeared in different forms and under the different titles ('budgies' and 'untitled') in *blart*, *3AM Magazine*, *e-ratio*, *Gammag*, *Sunfish*, and *Shadowtrain*. Thanks to the editors.

Special thanks are due to Peter Jaeger and Jeff Hilson.